Wheatfields Junior School
Downes Road, St. Albans
Herts AL4 9NT
01727 757443
www.wheatfieldsjm.herts.sch.uk

BLAZERS

GROSS JOBS in MEDICINE

by Nikki Bruno

raintree
a Capstone company — publishers for children

Raintree is an imprint of Capstone Global Library Limited, a company incorporated in England and Wales having its registered office at 264 Banbury Road, Oxford, OX2 7DY – Registered company number: 6695582

www.raintree.co.uk
myorders@raintree.co.uk

Text © Capstone Global Library Limited 2019
The moral rights of the proprietor have been asserted.

All rights reserved. No part of this publication may be reproduced in any form or by any means (including photocopying or storing it in any medium by electronic means and whether or not transiently or incidentally to some other use of this publication) without the written permission of the copyright owner, except in accordance with the provisions of the Copyright, Designs and Patents Act 1988 or under the terms of a licence issued by the Copyright Licensing Agency, Barnard's Inn, 86 Fetter Lane, London, EC4A 1EN (www.cla.co.uk). Applications for the copyright owner's written permission should be addressed to the publisher.

Edited by Hank Musolf
Designed by Bobbie Nuytten
Original illustrations © Capstone Global Library Limited 2019
Picture research by Heather Mauldin
Production by Katy LaVigne
Originated by Capstone Global Library Ltd
Printed and bound in India

ISBN 978 1 4747 7509 0
22 21 20 19 18
10 9 8 7 6 5 4 3 2 1

British Library Cataloguing in Publication Data
A full catalogue record for this book is available from the British Library.

Acknowledgements
We would like to thank the following for permission to reproduce photographs: iStockphoto: bitterfly, 12, Chris Ryan, 25, drbimages, 10-11, fstop123, 20-21, jxfzsy, 26-27, STEEX, 26 (inset), Steve Debenport, 14-15, 23, 24, 28-29, watanyou, 18; Shutterstock: ALPA PROD, cover, 1, 13, AndreyPopov, 8-9, frank60, 8 (inset), kdshutterman, 4-5, rdonar, 20 (inset), Romaset, 7, siamionau pavel, 19, Smeilov Sergey, 16-17. Design Elements: Shutterstock: Alhovik, Intel.nl, kasha_mala, Katsiaryna Chumakova, Yellow Stocking.

Every effort has been made to contact copyright holders of material reproduced in this book. Any omissions will be rectified in subsequent printings if notice is given to the publisher.

All the internet addresses (URLs) given in this book were valid at the time of going to press. However, due to the dynamic nature of the internet, some addresses may have changed, or sites may have changed or ceased to exist since publication. While the author and publisher regret any inconvenience this may cause readers, no responsibility for any such changes can be accepted by either the author or the publisher.

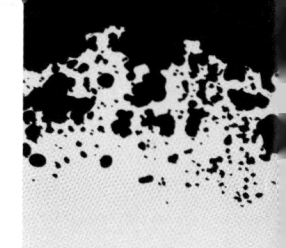

CONTENTS

Messy work in medicine 4
Ear, nose and throat doctor 6
Dermatologist 8
Fart smeller 10
Hospital laundry worker 12
Paramedic 14
Podiatrist 16
Dental hygienist 18
Wound care specialist 20
Nurse 22
A&e cleaner 24
Pathologist 26
Thank you medical workers! 28

    Glossary 30
    Find out more 31
    Index 32

MESSY WORK IN MEDICINE

Medical workers save lives every day. But some of them have to get gross on the job. Medical workers clean oozing cuts. They wash sheets soaked in wee. They help people who have been in bloody accidents.

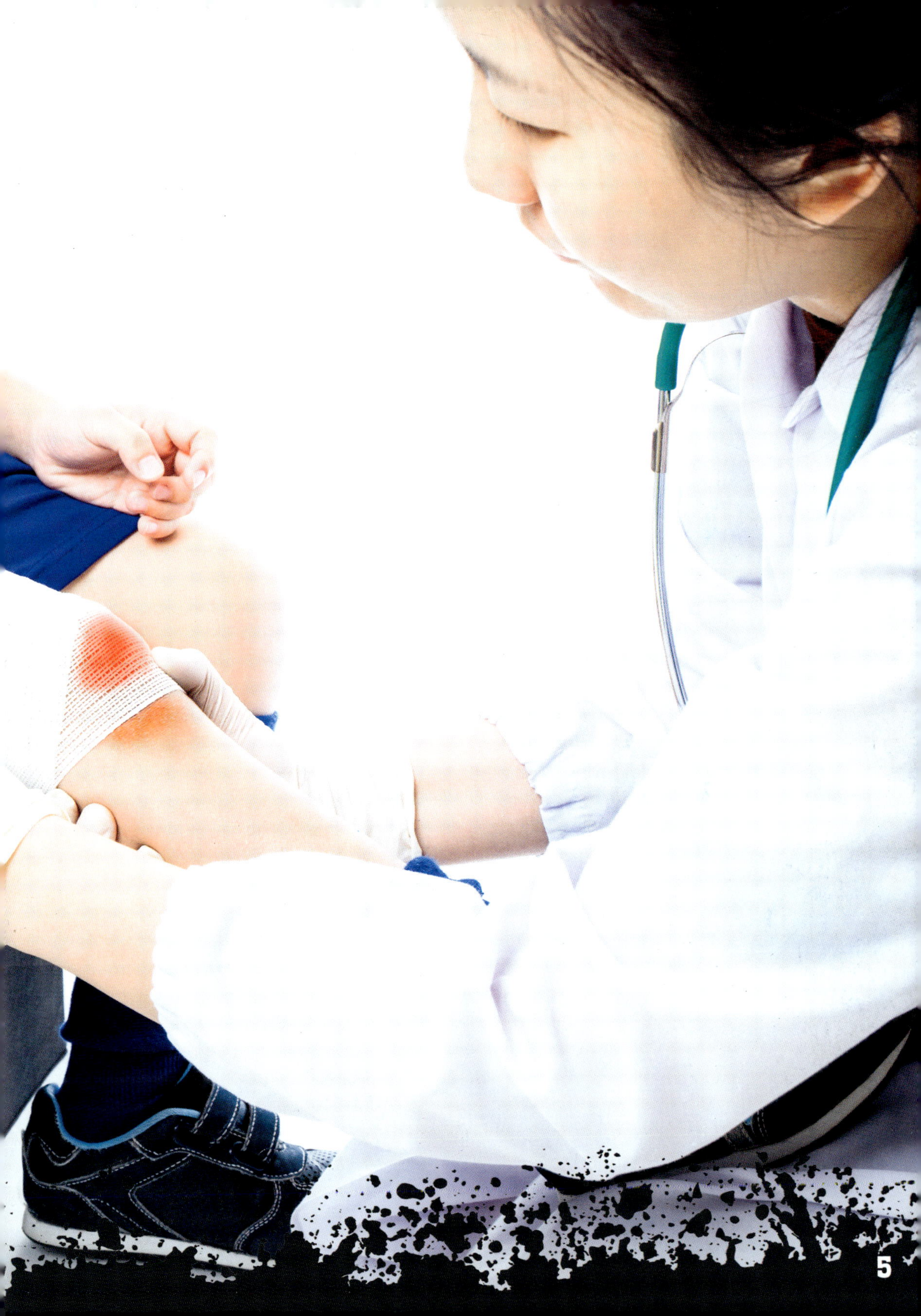

EAR, NOSE AND THROAT DOCTOR

What's inside ears, noses and throats? Earwax, snot and **saliva**! Ear, nose and throat doctors get close to these bodily fluids. They deal with **infected** body parts every day.

GROSS-O-METER

DID YOU KNOW?

Green or yellow snot usually means a person is fighting an infection.

saliva clear liquid in the mouth
infected filled with germs or viruses

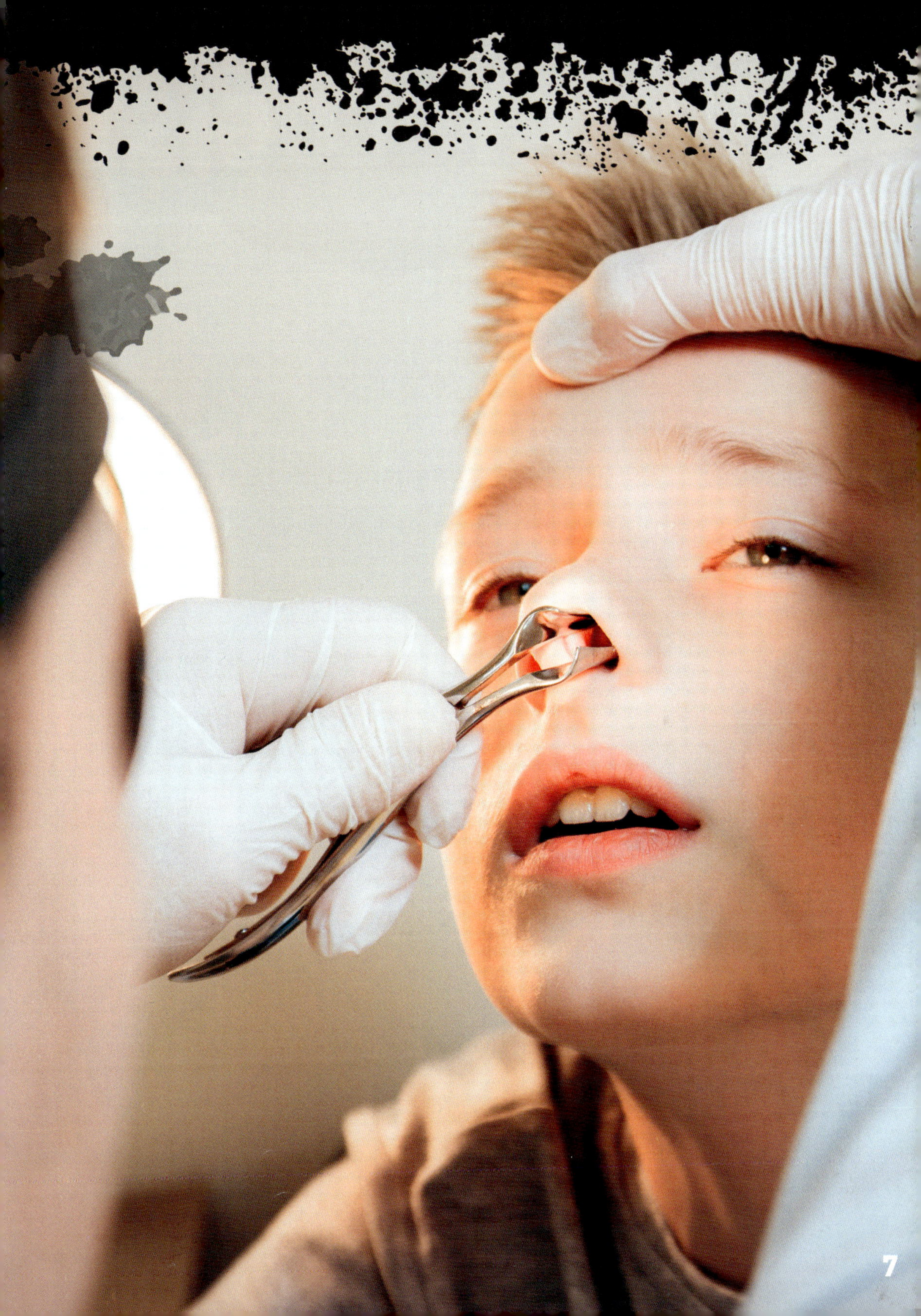

DERMATOLOGIST

Dermatologists are skin doctors. They treat spots. They drain smelly **pus** from sacs in the skin called **cysts**. One patient might have a crusty rash. Another might have a wound filled with tiny worms.

GROSS-O-METER

DID YOU KNOW?
Some people think foods such as chocolate and crisps can cause spots. This isn't true.

pus yellowish-white fluid found in sores and infections

cyst small sac that fills with fluid inside the skin

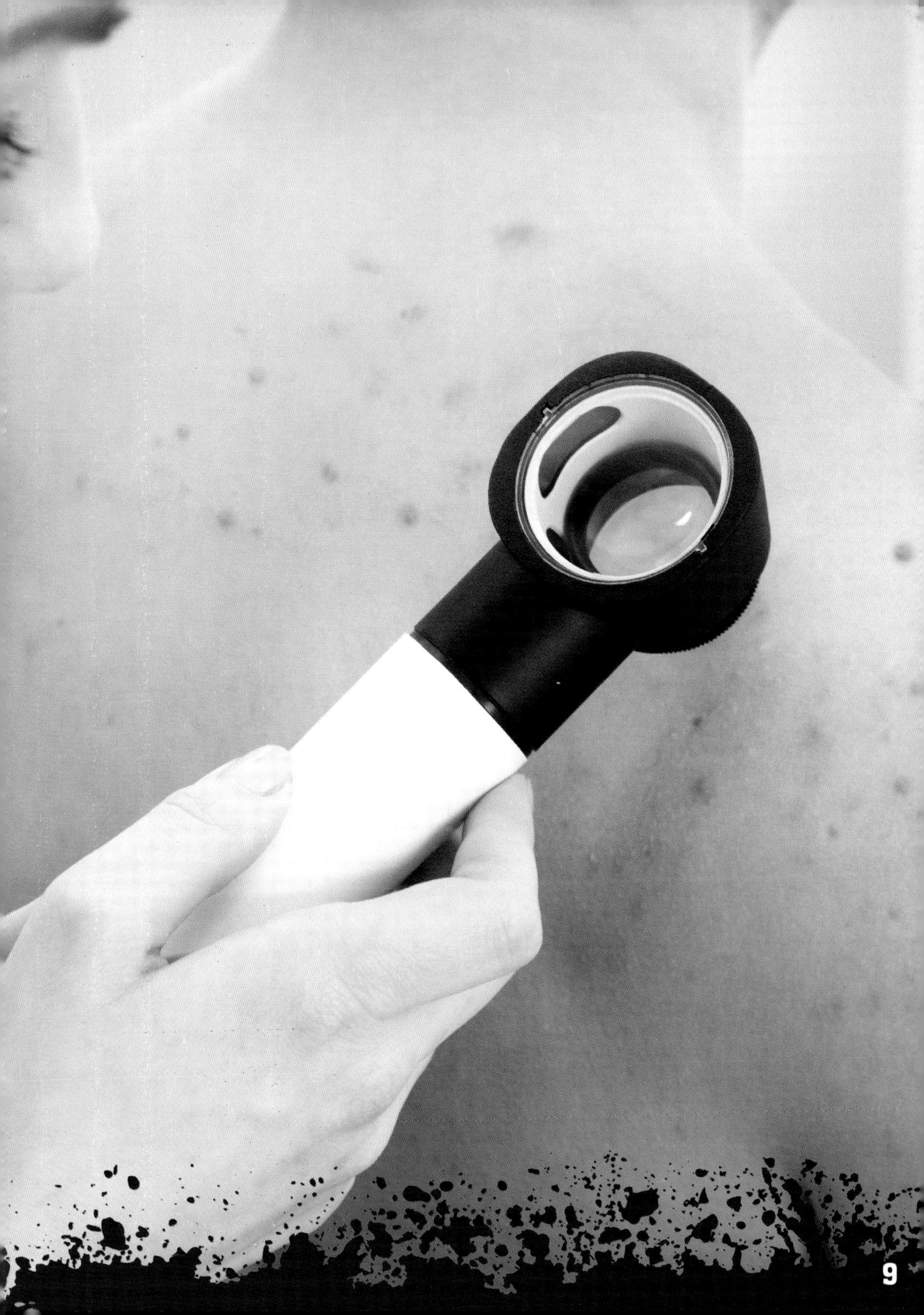

FART SMELLER

In China people actually get paid to smell farts! These workers have expert noses. A strong smell might mean the person has an infection. Professional fart smellers can even tell what a person eats!

GROSS-O-METER

DID YOU KNOW?

A fart smeller in China can make £40,000 per year.

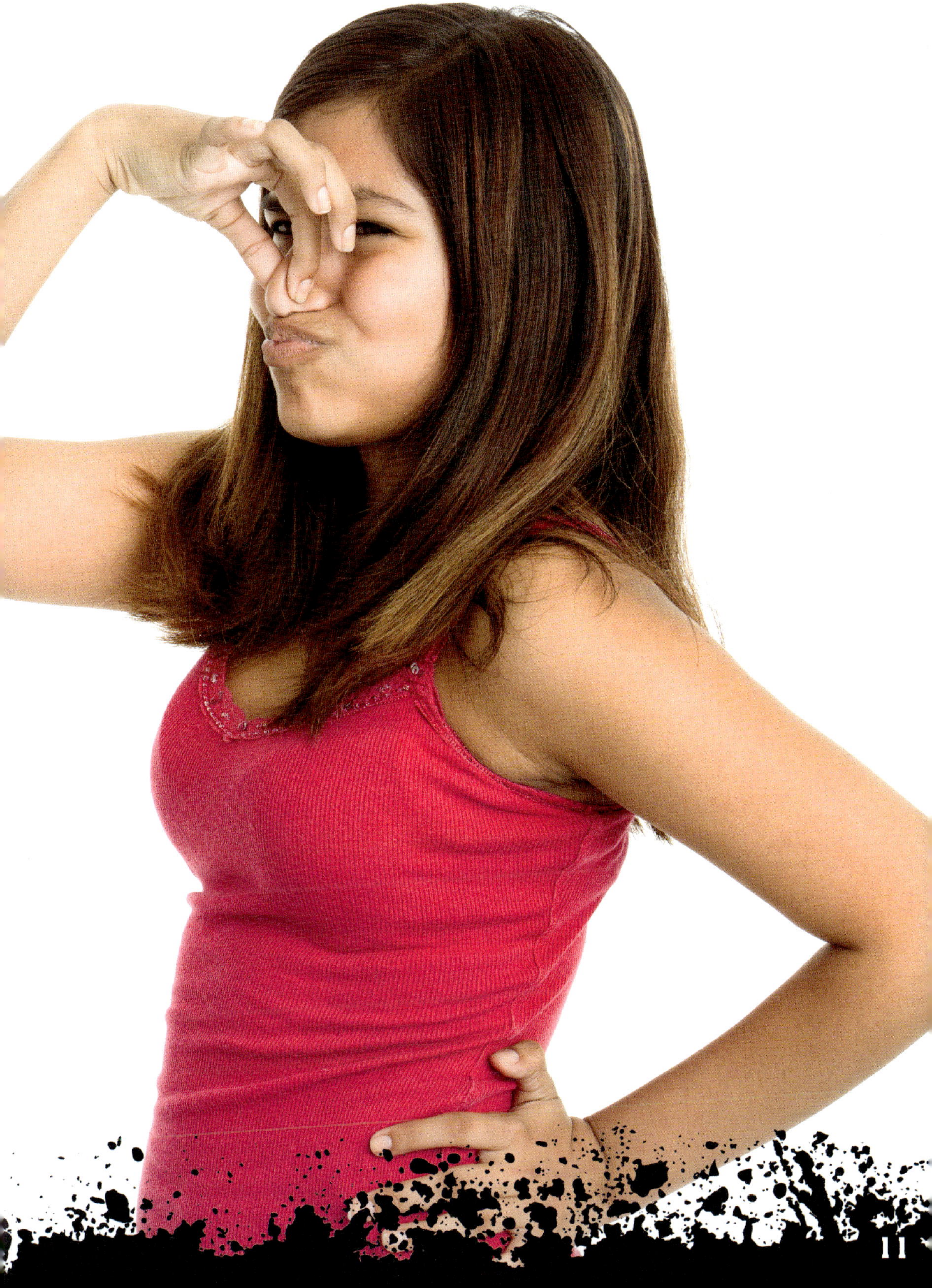

HOSPITAL LAUNDRY WORKER

Hospital laundry workers treat a lot more than grass stains. They clean huge piles of dirty, stinky sheets and clothes. They have to see and smell blood, vomit, wee, snot and poo.

GROSS-O-METER

DID YOU KNOW?

Germs from patients with diseases can stay on hospital sheets. Hospital laundry workers are more likely to get some diseases than other people.

germ tiny living thing that can cause sickness

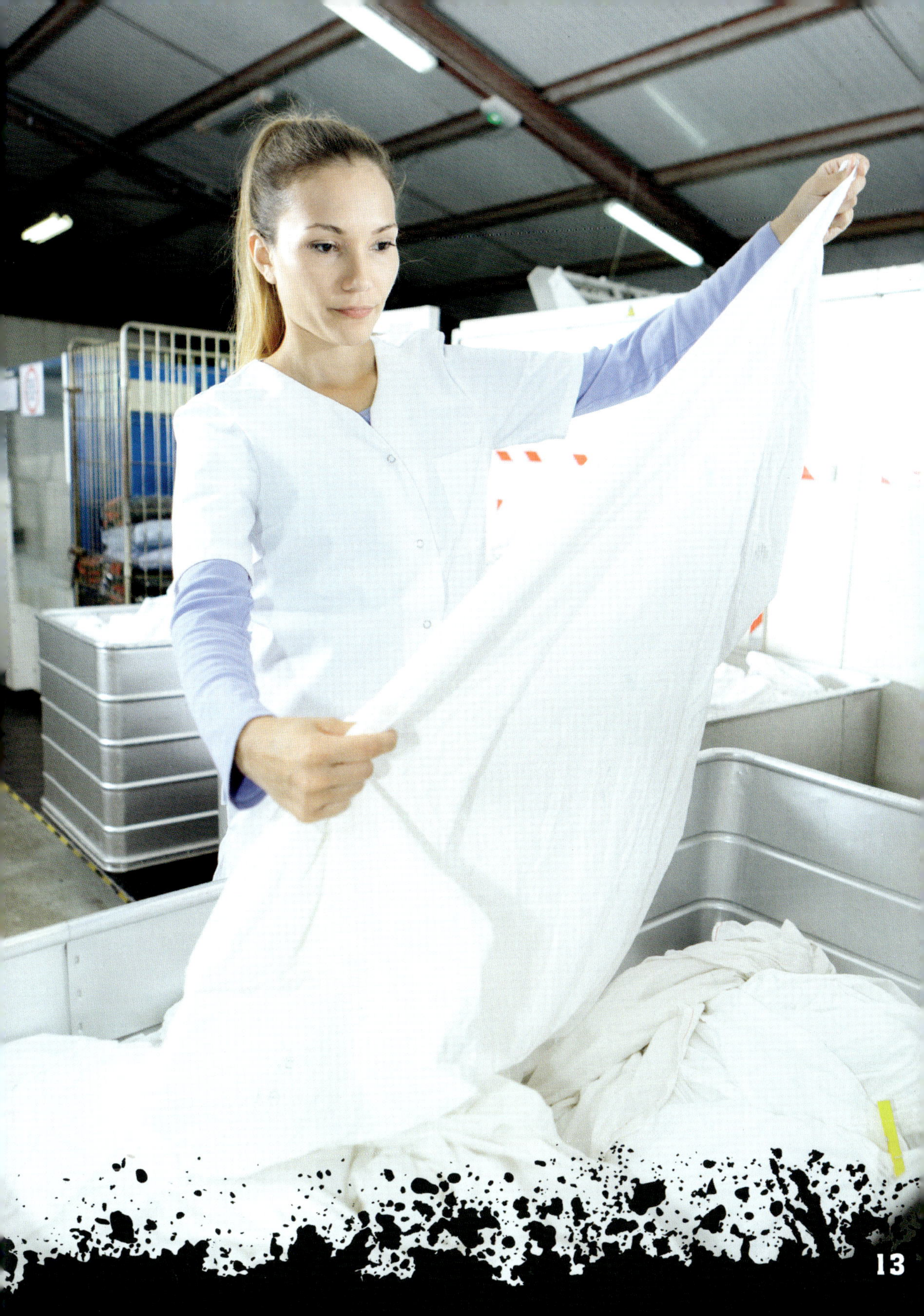

PARAMEDIC

Paramedics work for the ambulance service. These workers respond first to emergencies and accidents. Paramedics treat people who have been in car accidents. They also help women giving birth. Paramedics deal with blood and other bodily fluids.

GROSS-O-METER

DID YOU KNOW?
The ambulance service in England attended 6.6 million people in the year 2015–2016.

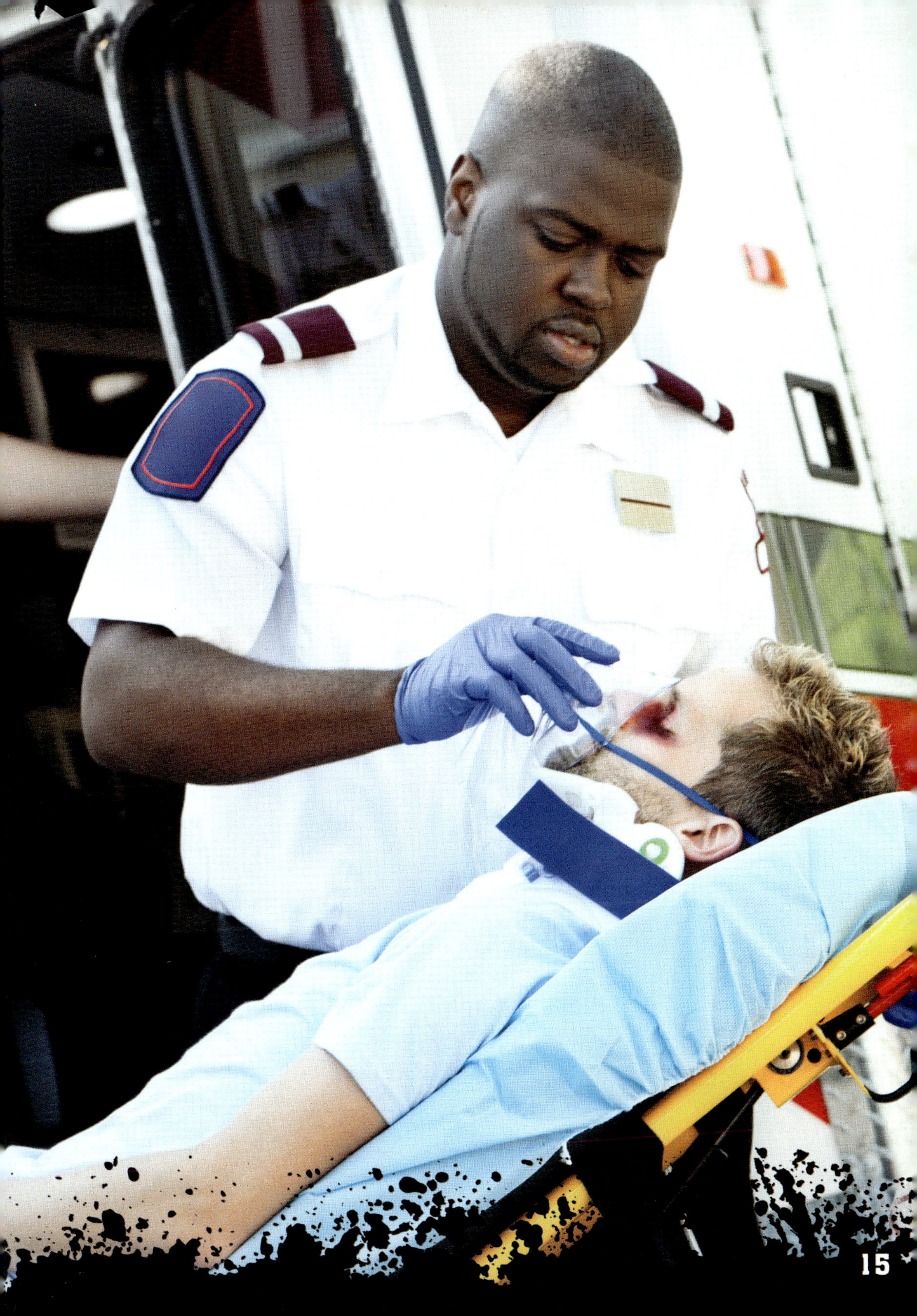

PODIATRIST

Feet do a lot of hard work, and they get very smelly. They may get a disgusting **fungus** called athlete's foot. Sometimes **warts** grow on them. Podiatrists are foot doctors. They treat these conditions and many more.

NAIL FUNGUS

Nail fungus can grow on toenails. Toenails with fungus turn yellow. Sometimes they chip off and crumble. The best treatment is medicine taken by mouth.

GROSS-O-METER

fungus living thing similar to a plant, but without flowers, leaves or green colouring; some types of fungus cause disease

wart small, hard growth on the skin, often caused by a virus

17

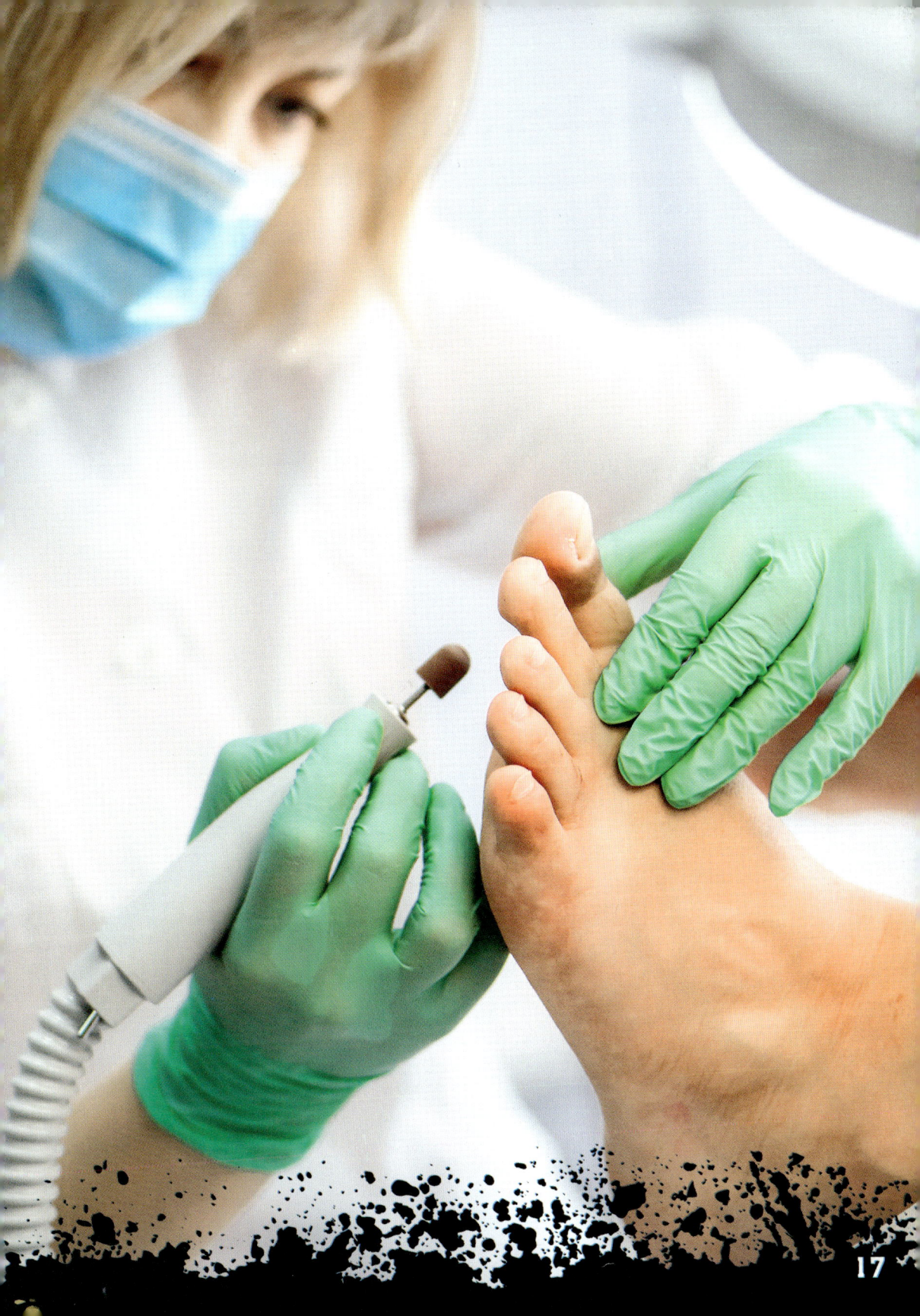

DENTAL HYGIENIST

Bad breath, bloody gums and yellow teeth are on anyone's gross list. A dental **hygienist** deals with these every day. This person's job is to clean teeth and gums.

GROSS-O-METER

DID YOU KNOW?

Gingivitis is a type of gum disease. It makes gums puffy and red. Dental hygienists see it a lot. They tell people how to prevent this disease.

hygienist person who is trained to help a dentist; hygienists clean teeth and take X-rays

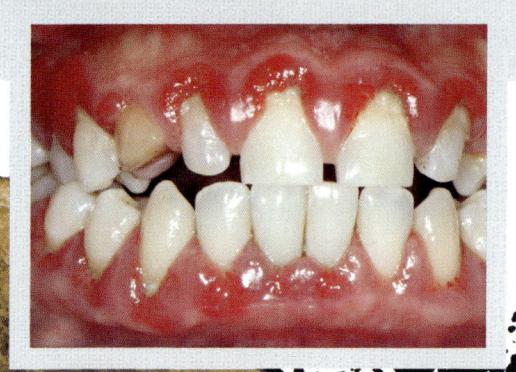

19

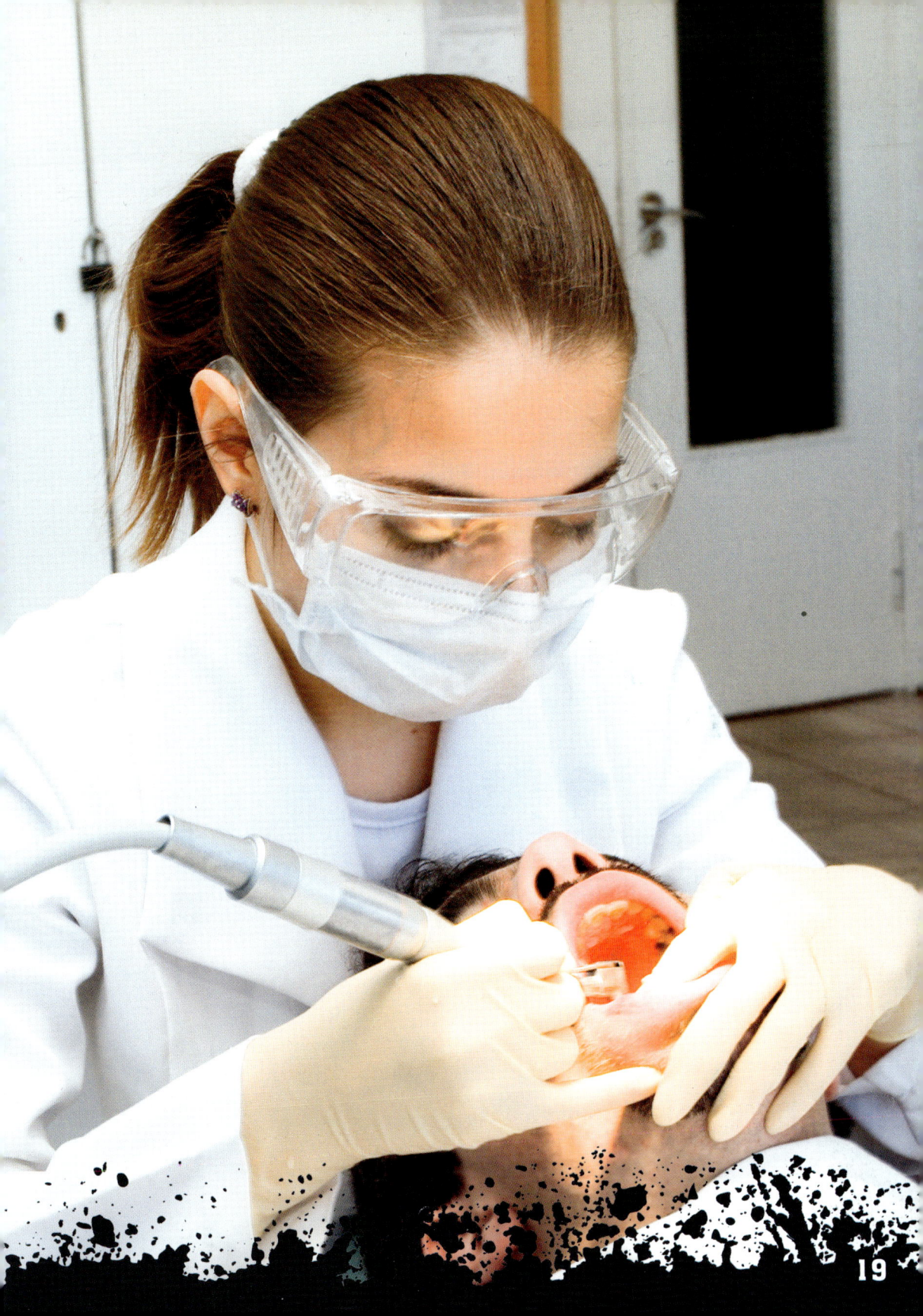

WOUND CARE SPECIALIST

Wound care specialists work in hospitals and clinics. They clean, treat and wrap cuts, burns and other injuries. Blood, pus and awful smells are part of the job. The older the wound, the nastier it usually is.

DID YOU KNOW?

Wound care specialists sometimes have to remove skin from an infected wound. This helps it heal.

GROSS-O-METER

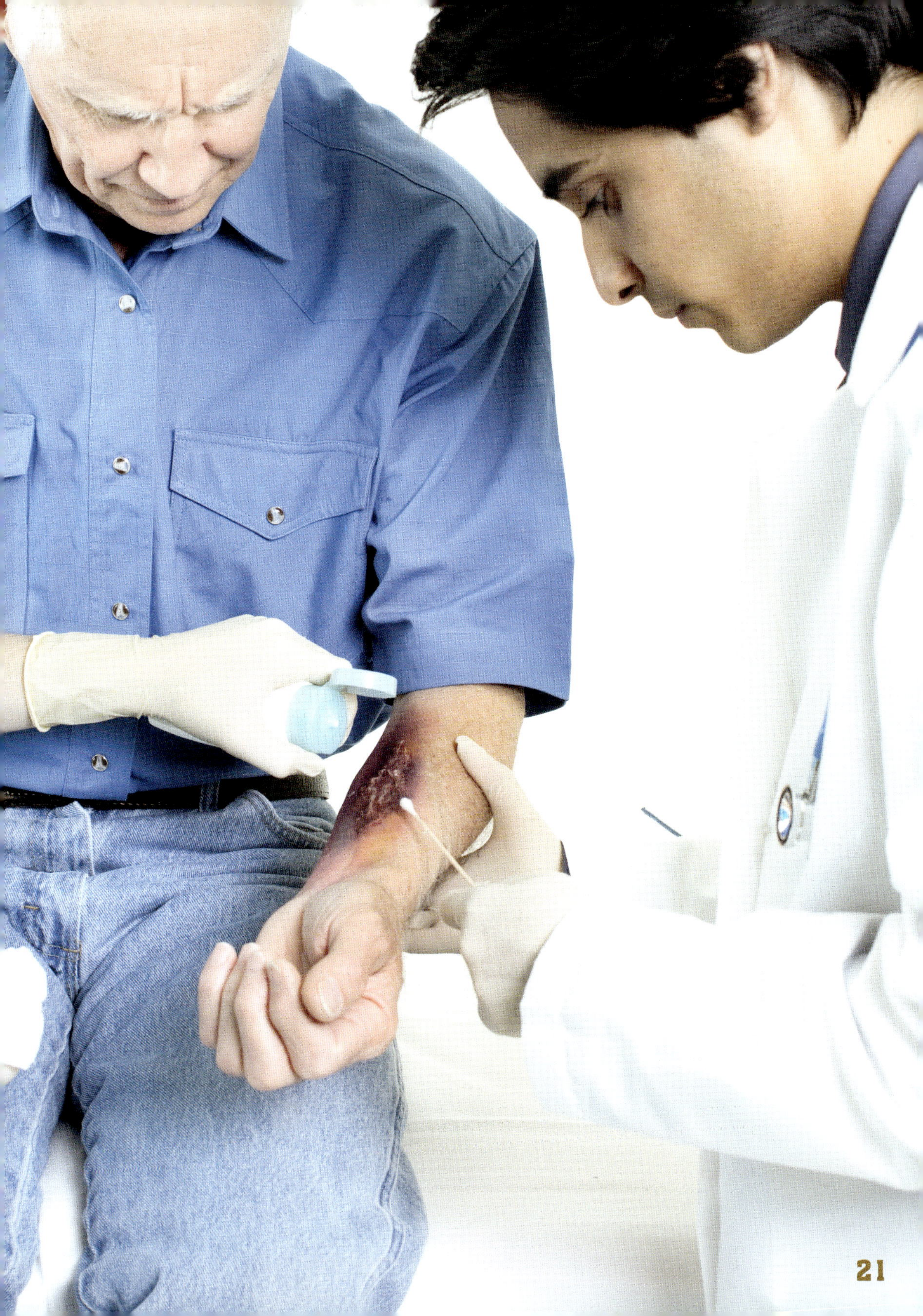

NURSE

Nurses treat patients and help doctors in operations. They deal with everything that can come out of a person. They get covered with all types of bodily fluids and waste. Even nurses get grossed out. Sometimes they leave the patient's room to be sick.

GROSS-O-METER

DID YOU KNOW?
Sometimes people are unable to wash themselves at home. Nurses may need to bathe new patients who haven't washed in months.

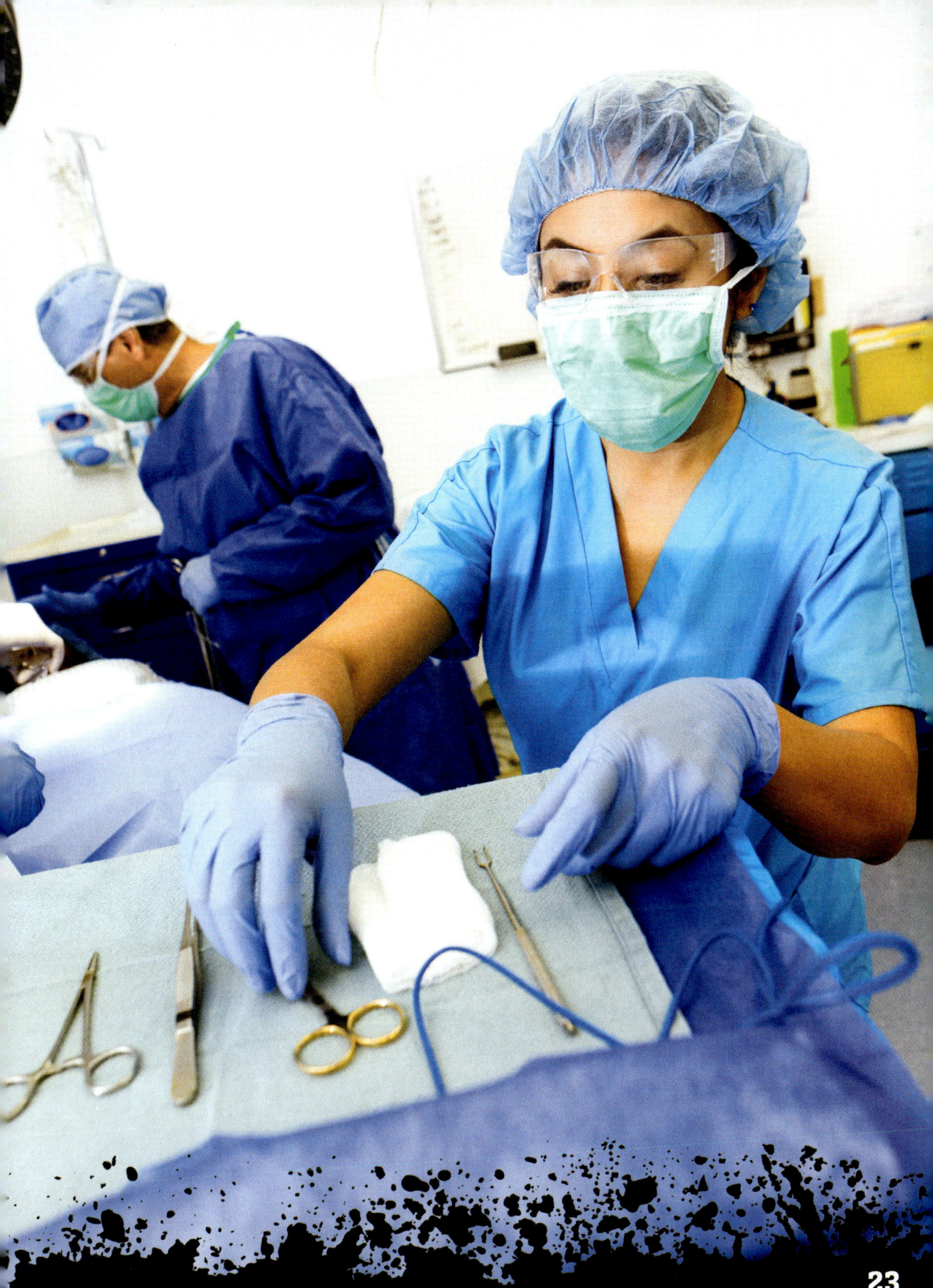

A&E CLEANER

Accident and Emergency (A&E) departments get messy. Patients there are very sick or badly injured. A&E cleaners clear up the messes left behind. That could mean blood, vomit, body **tissue** and more.

DID YOU KNOW?

In 2017–2018, 23.8 million people visited A&E departments in England.

GROSS-O-METER

tissue layer or bunch of soft material that makes up body parts

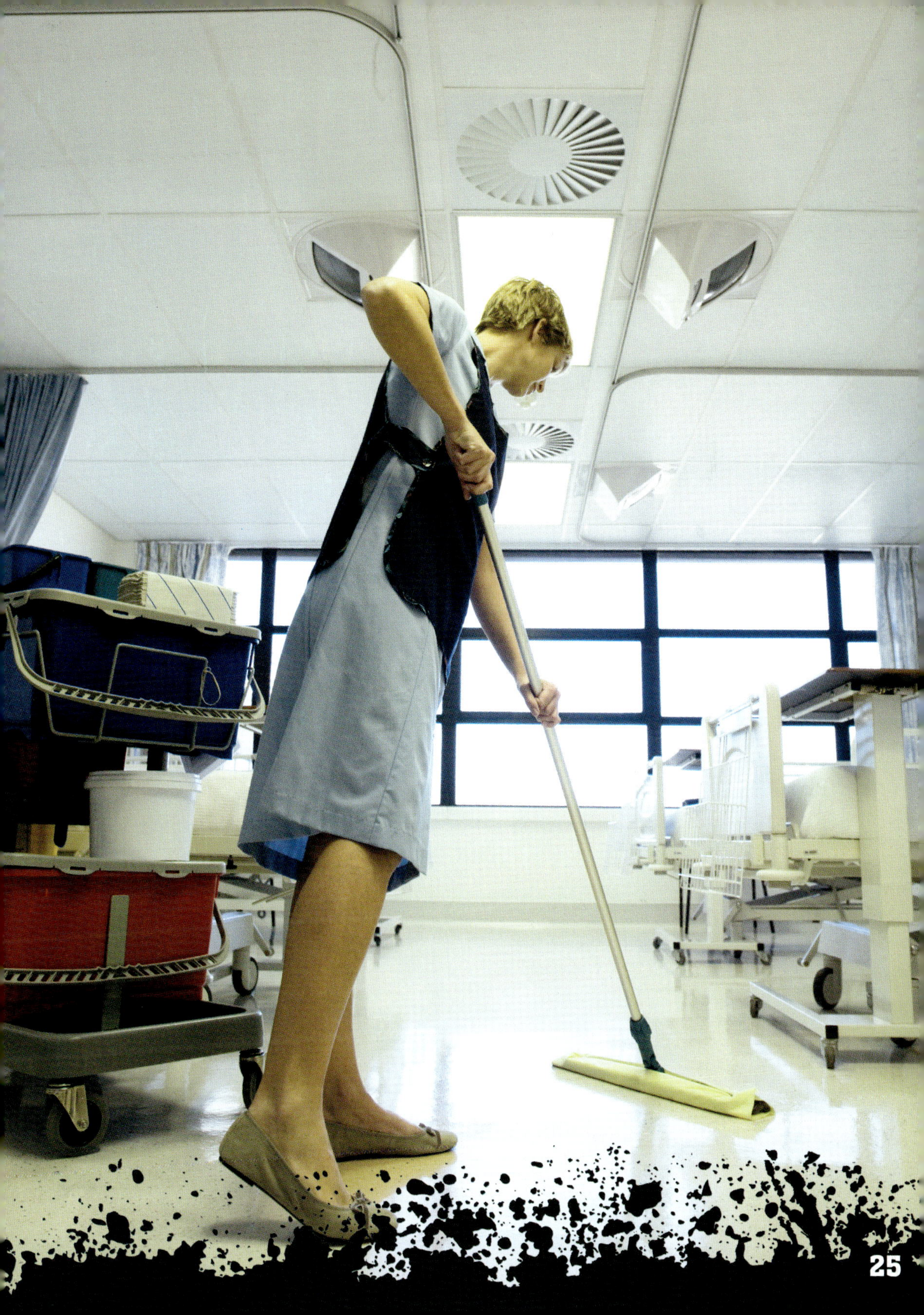

PATHOLOGIST

Pathologists are disease detectives. They search for sickness and poisons in the body. They spend lots of time looking through a **microscope**. These workers study blood, wee and body tissue.

MICRO-TECH

Pathologists use expensive microscopes to find diseases. There are many different types of microscope. Some are good for looking at blood. Others are best for looking at tissue.

microscope tool that makes very small things look large enough to be seen

26

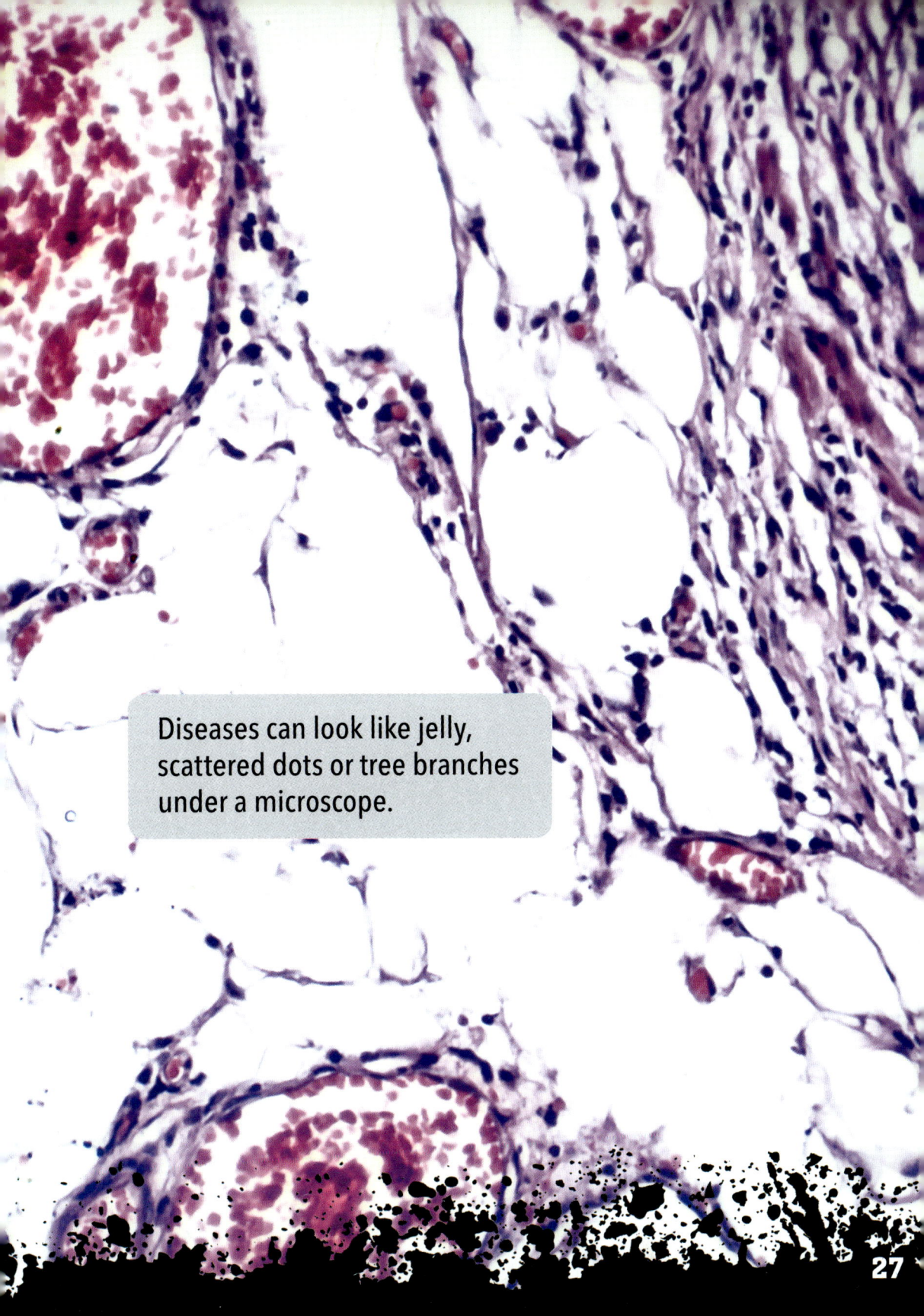

Diseases can look like jelly, scattered dots or tree branches under a microscope.

THANK YOU MEDICAL WORKERS!

Human life would be so much harder without medical workers. These heroes treat and cure diseases. They keep doctors' surgeries and hospitals clean. But they certainly do have dirty jobs!

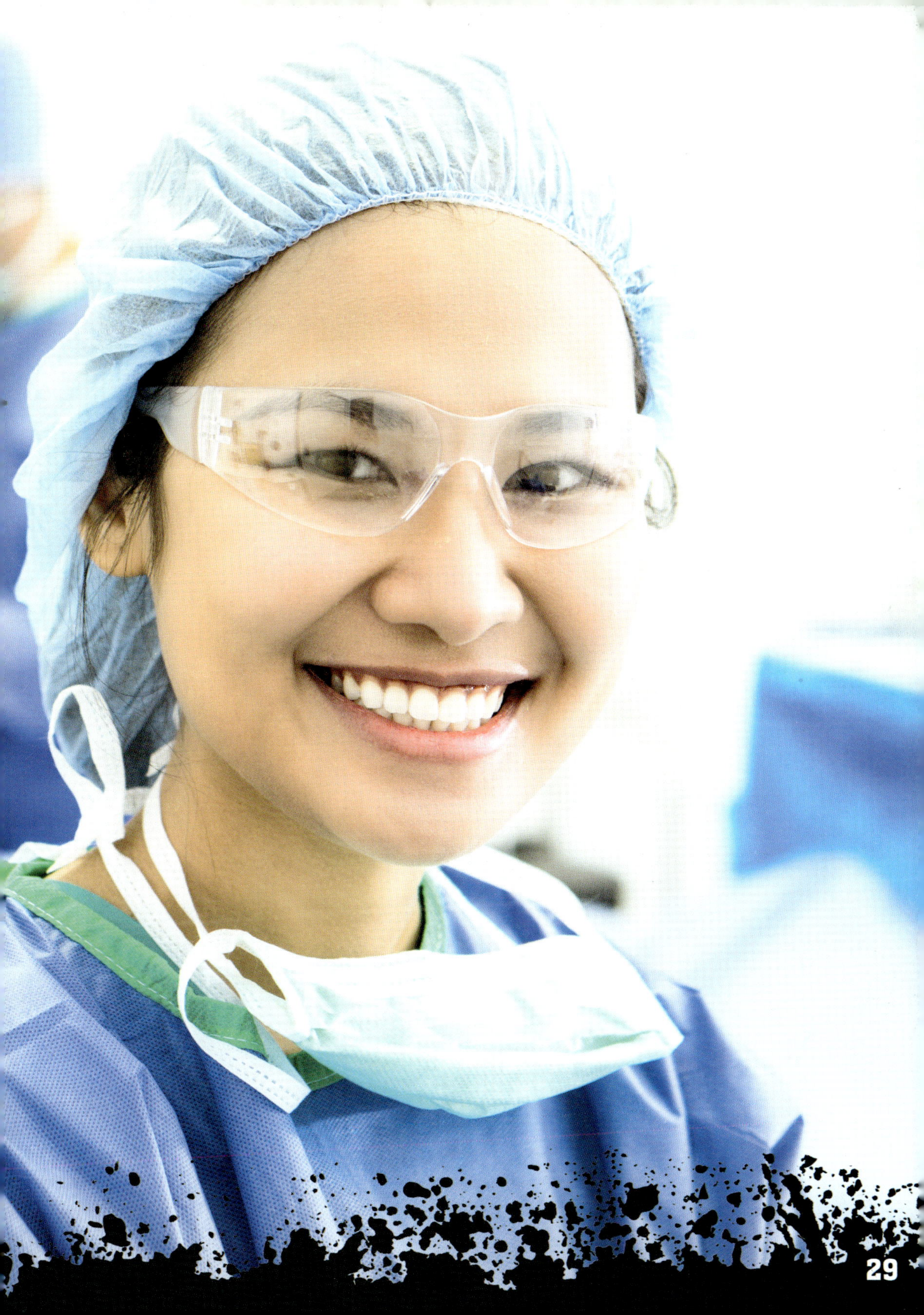

GLOSSARY

cyst small sac that fills with fluid inside the skin

fungus living thing similar to a plant, but without flowers, leaves or green colouring; some types of fungus cause disease

germ tiny living thing that can cause sickness

hygienist person who is trained to help a dentist; hygienists clean teeth and take X-rays

infected filled with germs or viruses

microscope tool that makes very small things look large enough to be seen

pus yellowish-white fluid found in sores and infections

saliva clear liquid in the mouth

tissue layer or bunch of soft material that makes up body parts

wart small, hard growth on the skin, often caused by a virus

FIND OUT MORE
BOOKS

Blood, Bones and Body Bits (Horrible Science), Nick Arnold (Scholastic, 2018)

Science (Jobs If You Like…), Charlotte Guillain (Raintree, 2013)

Your Skin and Bones (Your Body By Numbers), Melanie Waldron (Raintree, 2014)

WEBSITES

www.bbc.co.uk/schools/0/ww1/25403868
Learn about some medical heroes from World War I.

www.dkfindout.com/uk/human-body
Find out more about the human body.

INDEX

blood 4, 12, 14, 18, 20, 24, 26

cuts 4, 20
cysts 8

diseases 12, 18, 26, 28

earwax 6

farts 10
fungi 16

infections 6, 10, 20

laundry 12

microscopes 28

pus 8, 20

rashes 8

saliva 6
snot 6, 12
spots 8

teeth 18
tissue 24, 26

vomit 12, 24

warts 16
worms 8
wounds 8, 20